I0192052

Neruda's Memoirs

poems

Maureen E. Doallas

ts T. S. Poetry Press • New York

T. S. Poetry Press
Ossining, New York
Tspoetry.com

© 2011 by Maureen E. Doallas

This work is licensed under the Creative Commons Attribution-Share Alike 3.0 United States License. To view a copy of this license, visit http://creativecommons.org/licenses/by-sa/3.0/us/ or send a letter to Creative Commons, 171 Second Street, Suite 300, San Francisco, California 94105, USA.

Reference is made in various pieces in this collection to the following brands and sources: *Alice in Wonderland: An IMAX 3D Experience* is a film by Tim Burton, Walt Disney Pictures, based on Lewis Carroll's *Alice's Adventures in Wonderland; Barbie* is a product of Mattel, Inc.; *Chanel* is a Parisian fashion house; *Goodnight Moon* is a children's book by Margaret Wise Brown, Harper Division of HarperCollins; *Harley-Davidson* is a product of Harley-Davidson Motor Company; *How Hour* is a term denoting the time a bomb detonates; *Jabberwocky* is a poem from Lewis Carroll's *Through the Looking Glass; Lucky Strike* is a product of Reynolds American, Inc.; *Mail Pouch* is a chewing tobacco product of Bloch Brothers Tobacco Company; *McDonald's* is a fast-food restaurant chain; *National Cancer Institute* is a division of the U.S. National Institutes of Health; *Pan Am* is the commonly known name for Pan American World Airways, which operated from 1927 to 1991; *Southern Comfort* is a product of Southern Comfort Company; "Southern Legitimacy Statement" and "School of Southern Literature" are from *The Dead Mule School of Southern Literature*, a literary journal; *U.S. Naval Observatory* is the official source of time for the U.S. Department of Defense and a standard of time for the United States; "War on Cancer" generally refers to the effort, initiated with the signing in 1971 of U.S. Public Law 92-218 (National Cancer Act), to find a cure for cancer; *The Washington Post* is a product of The Washington Post Company.

Scripture taken from the *Holy Bible, New International Version*. Copyright © 1973, 1978, 1984 International Bible Society. Used by Permission of Zondervan Bible Publishers.

Susan Neiman quotation from *Evil in Modern Thought*, Princeton University Press (2004); Ezra Pound quotation from *The Pisan Cantos (80/515)*; Rabindranath Tagore quotation from *Fireflies* (1928).

Cover image © by Randall David Tipton. Used by permission of the artist. http://www.randalldavidtipton.com/

ISBN 978-09845531-3-6

Library of Congress Cataloging-in-Publication Data:
Doallas, Maureen E.
        [Poems.]
        Neruda's Memoirs: Poems/Maureen E. Doallas
        ISBN 978-09845531-3-6
        Library of Congress-Control Number: 2011920594

The following poems appeared in different versions at the following venues or in the following publications: *TweetSpeakPoetry:* "We Can Remember"; *the sad red earth:* "Grief"; *Kalliope, A Journal of Women's Art* (The Florida Issue): "Crossing Alligator Alley: The Everglades at Dusk."

for Drew, because every son deserves a mother
who can trill like a poet

Contents

I.

Enter

I was born in Virginia, in the county where I live today, just outside
Washington, D.C. On first meeting me, people declaim the fact
that I'm "a native," forgetting, perhaps, that not all of us are politi-
cians, bi-coastals, or military. Excluding my college years in New
York and a six-month mistake of time in Florida, I've lived in no
other place I'd call home. I am, however, anything but Southern
and would have great trouble coming up with a "Southern Legiti-
macy Statement" were I asked to produce one for the "School of
Southern Literature."

Being a Northern Virginian, I could be said not to be of Vir-
ginia at all. I speak with no discernible regional accent, though I
swear my sisters in Georgia and Tennessee do. I've never driven a
pick-up with a rebel's decal displayed the length of the rear window,
nor have I shot and dressed deer, flown the Confederate flag, or
played the part of a re-enactor, except once, in a local Halloween
parade, I was an Indian maiden, my below-waist-length hair
braided, authentic beads laced round my neck, my feet in hand-
made moccasins. I've tried grits and hush puppies both, will not
drink sweet tea, have never enjoyed collards, or made a toddy of
Southern Comfort or sour mash. I never fry chicken or pull pork.

My roots do not go deep in my home state. My parents arrived
at The Plains, Virginia, from Massachusetts, two children in tow
and a third on the way. My mother's family was English and Irish,
long-living Protestants fighting with long-living Catholics. Not a
Baptist in the bunch. My father's family is unknown. An orphan
at four, he was a first-generation Greek-American who had
no opportunities but what he made of his hard life himself,
and he talked the salty language of men who worked farms
before warring in the mountains of China, the snake-in-
fested jungles of Burma, and the fetid rivers of India. He
never went beyond grade eight but showed wisdom impos-
sible to find in books. What he acquired in service to his

country as a member of the "Greatest Generation" he knew to put to use. He sent North for his chewing tobacco: *Mail Pouch*.

I grew up enamored of Abraham Lincoln whose "Gettysburg Address" I memorized and recited to win honors. Due south of where I lived, a statue of a Confederate soldier reminded me never to make much of that fact. A source of Southern pride, that statue remains erect in the middle of a heavily-traveled highway in the center of a city whose streets bear names like Duke and Prince and Princess, a place with a colonial past where not a few "Beltway Bandits," like their mostly liberty-loving predecessors of hundreds of years past, make home, acting as if they were born here.

Trouble in Paradise

1

Eve, flowing hair so gold, so soft,
would sit amidst grass
at water's edge, gazing,
mostly wondering.

Hoping to read the clouds
another morning,
she looked to sun for solace,
bent an ear to hear the music.

Showy birds in boughs
did turn the landscape red.

Sky so bright as tin
did distort for her
his heart beat.

Adam, going nowhere,
read the signs well:
Love is dead
where roses pale.

Looking for such bright fruit
Eve denied,
Adam, as he dared,
wandered
to satisfy
his quaking hunger.

2

Hope rises
another morning.

Once more she bid
to see him,
once more did greet him.

Eve, hair flowing,
bid Adam come closer
one final good night.

3

Hope falls.
A heart beat
not heard
by one not loved
loses meaning.

Eve fights with words,
to get word out:

Like a whisper
never heard.

4

A freight of words
weighs down
meaning,

and Eve prefers
poems and prayers.

Fragments of words
sound as tin,
distort her reasoning,
leave her no good words
on which to fall
back in love.

5

Signs of loss:
the ashy fragment of a wasp's nest
bird's wing torn
roses pale
black leaves
the landscape red
the sky black.

6

Eve (as usual),
she thought of Adam,
how he left her
crumbs and ashes.

7

Lips twisting, curling,
jawbone held tight,

words escape the mouth,
twist the tongue,
sometimes shame.

Every black note
she hit did resound.

8

Having known a thousand ways
round him,
she makes her point
a new night's play
at water's edge.

In her tall blue Chinese jar
she put elixir
for nights long, for nights dark,
mixed cloves and thyme
sticks of cinnamon
with rose petals
eggshells so delicate
bird's wing torn
the ashy fragment of a wasp's nest
bad memories.

9

By evening
silver fish send up a clue.

10

Those who witnessed
saw how Adam
turned his back,
and back against the wind,
never heard.

She began to sing
a song of wanting,
of Adam
another morning.

Hazardous Duty: Ode to My Kitchen

I have no taste
for the violence
my kitchen demands of me

to squeeze and score
fillet and fry
flash-freeze and melt

ground grind and grill
mash whip whisk
or beat till stiff.

I conscientiously object
to chopping things to bits
when it's enough

to simply pare away peel back
or toss and throw together
what's simmered steamed or stewed.

But ask me for my recipes
and I'll tell you:
not just any Bloody Mary will do.

Learning to Communicate

Go ahead,
now!

Trace that line
of thought

between your first point
and your next

and be prepared
to scrimmage.

I know you know
somewhere

down the line
somebody's always ready

to draw a line
to hold a line

to bring you
into line.

That's *not* my line.

So drop it!
Don't take that line

with me.
For once

put yourself on the line
and stand

where I stand:
on no line

not in the line of duty.

I know you know
you have to

get out
of line

to cross a line
to see

how a line
can curve

can cut in
then go out again

even before
too fine

a line gets made.

Yes, we all have
to take a turn

getting back
in line

with what's expected.

But first
give me

any line you want;
spin it out

and reel it back.
You're sure to line up

with the best of 'em
so long as you vow

to keep the line open.

Art Lecture 101

In a nursing home
nobody wants to hear
that old news
about Picasso's Blue Period.

Blue's a color
they get too well
after their last visitor's gone.

Mondrian's neatly divided
blocks of big strong
reds and greens and yellows

won't do, either,
sorry to say.

After a while,
minds tend to lose hold
of one compartment after another.

Kandinsky?
A reject, too.

So many circles,
like the halls they roam after hours,
once the meals are done,
leave them dizzy
going nowhere.

Well, how about Chagall,
then?

Girls on goats,
houses high in air,
figures floating
with feet off ground!

Perfect,
they stir at last:

Dreamscapes,
like the final kiss
they remember giving
the one they love.

Burn Out

funny
how the mind
works up
the challenge
to clear
a space

one minute
scouting
distance to go
the phoenix
rising
from the nook
of ash, embers
streaming live
wires
still

the next
sentenced
to map
the terrain
of the broken
warp and weft
over and under
and crossed
connections
loosed

the mind's night
light
its own
and only
swaddle
surface wrap
a layer plumped
against the too-high
too-fast
climb

Gone to Seed

Fireweed done producing,
gone to seed,

brilliance cuts a swath
through green's shallowing shelter.

Agitated Monet yellows
burnished van Gogh reds:
two nods to nature's talents.

Lips of leaves
crisp
curl
cascade.

I carry a palette that can't compete
with summer's last firing.

If I'm lucky,
my hand will find its way
before the final fall.

Crossing Alligator Alley: The Everglades at Dusk

This land, it's fit for nothing
but beauty, and you pay to cross it.

Flat green palmetto parades
a stubby quilt of fans.

Sawgrass stiffens, erecting itself
like a spine mastered in ballet class.

Gray-as-bone Spanish moss hangs limp,
suggesting how a man holds his head in shame.

Brittle-barked Australian pine, skyscraper of shade,
intrudes worse than a visitor on Sunday.

It's the heat urging you on,
and concrete heaving broken blisters.

Lazy-eyed storms don't happen this far south.
Only water moves at a dying pitch, algaed in setting sun.

Where this place starves of habit,
wind breaks of song. Silence stalls.

Danger waits conspicuous, makes do
with quiet repetitions.

But secrets are no big deal here.

Vultures moody-beaked and smooth of face
track events with a vengeance.

Joy-Waiting in Advent

Yes-blessed
wind-rushed
Gabriel out-breathes

Suddenly it's done
Mary with One
to-be birth

With haste
to greet to press to rub
palm against cheek
cheek against hand
hand against belly

Hand to hand in hand
with haste
two to meeting make

Mary with Elizabeth too
each Holy Spirit-touched each

One carrying one
receiving the One giving
the blessing of joy-waiting

Blessed Joy turning
swelling leaping
for joy waiting for Joy
held in heart
times two

Blessed refuge
womb-sheltered
in Word blessed

In sacred song
Joy-waiting One
One Joy-waiting
Joy waiting

A Mother-To-Be in Waiting

In the space between
the waiting
and the coming

there is moonlight
given to morning.

Breaths held
released
now holding

soon seek
to give light
to give life
to give love

What It Costs

No thing in life
is just
for the asking.

Dead-heading
always follows
the first hard freeze.

Rivers
break banks
with too much rain.

Sparrows leave
nests empty
when owls fly.

Night-thoughts
I can't call dreams.

Taking Leave

He asked,
What will you have
on New Year's Eve?

Two eggs over
on cinnamon toast,
bacon on the side.

She didn't count
on the pan
going missing.

Love Not Love

1

Worry
what he takes
as just a silly little feud

his lust
your wanting

work out like this:

even with the furs
traded as down-payment
he'll leave you cold

2

Eyes roving
hitting
missing (mostly)

wander-lust
leaves a trail
with no followers

3

She was warned
he wouldn't stand
for ceremony

She got silk words
surface polished to shiny

So great a luster
for her
didn't disappoint

It's a matter
of choice after all

4

He thrummed desire
with the speed of a clock
striking down seconds

Love you, she'd say
her heart
invisibly indivisible

his beat unsoothed
scanning giver then receiver

proof enough

love goes
so far
so far
so far

What I really like

is how words
aren't needed

to hold in mind

the slant the sun takes
when it pitches
a fit

of rays on the sea
at dusk

or the cut-through line
at the horizon's edge

once you've pulled back
and turned
for one last look

at the world

you've traveled to
and through

to reach home.

How Arguments Go

1

Pieces never tell the whole story.
Safety glass still breaks;
it just doesn't shatter.

Heat escapes through clear glass,
its pattern unseen in fragments
but no less visible.

Opaque glass,
like shades pulled against sun,
hides what most any fool can catch in light.

2

She's got her side. He's got his.

Chipped words go air-borne
when thrown against the mirror.

Clean-up happens by fits and starts.

3

Cuts can be on the surface,
unremarked,
or slide slickly along fault lines.

Sometimes it takes a probe
and a camera's eye to show you
what you're looking for.

4

Windows in wind rattle,
at night shadow

Roughed edges
slivers
the dog's bone half-consumed.

See Me, Let Me, Be Me *Barbie*

See me be:

Anemone Barbie in my Christian Louboutin.

I'm inspired, like the ad says, head-to-toe,
done up nice in my lime green with pretty purple bow.

Shall I channel Nefertiti? Maybe Marilyn Monroe?
Get a quick make-over before my next show?

Limit. Five babes per order. While supplies last.
I'm va-va-voom in a catsuit, too, and fast.

Let me be:

Your *Fantasy Barbie*, say, *The Scarlet Macaw*.

Lavishly embellished in striking red shantung,
I can be anyone's bright vision, real top-of-the-rung.

The picture of perfection. Such a deal! I glow.
I come with my very own parrot and a dress cut low.

Arrgh. Away with you, *Pirate Barbie*, with your better deal.
One look at your price tells 'em I'm no steal.

But I admit you're arresting in your swashbucklin' style,
buckled boots, brocade coat, gold hoop earring, no bile.

Velvet breeches, some ruffles, and lots of lace,
such fancy frocks play up your saucy buccaneer's face.

Be me:

I do that diversity thing oh so well.

There's the I that's *Miss Astronaut*
who sashays into space,

that *Black* beauty in afro and *Stylin' Hair Grace.*
There's the I can be *Barbra* or *Cyndi* or *Joan*

stepping out with Midge while Allan's alone.
I travel the world, I pack light as can be,

I'm *Eiffel Tower, Big Ben, Statue of Liberty.*
My theme's not just *France,* nor only *Italy.*

Need a *Registered Nurse?* No worries, you see;
I carry my accoutrements wherever I be.

For Pan Am I fly, and always first class.
Call me *Stewardess* once, I respond in a flash.

But a secret confession I do have to make,
I'm *Harley-Davidson Barbie* when I catch a brake.

Decked out in my finest white biker chic,
I can yell at the wind, I'm not meek! Not a freak!

Follow-Through

This place that he bequeathed to you,
you honored, word for word,
affixing loss once yours to ours
and naming thus what grief
kept close, could grow beyond.

You, far off the path by that canal
among the oaks he loved so well,
nourished us
until nourished we found our way.

Summer Camp Highlights

Blackberry pickings
Mouths filling, spilling
Purple, trickling stains

Hiking quilted brown-needled floors
Lightning bugs mapping flight paths
Sprays of pine rustling after-dinner songs

Scat sightings, owl watching
Hawk gliding, copper heads slithering
Rattlers beading alarms

Tin cup rumblings night checkings
Tent flaps flipping off silence
Sleeping bags joined

Arms unscreened going rage-red
Heat seeking water holes
Pent-up boyness letting go

Castoffs

Do you remember what we promised when we met
　　　meaning forever to promise keep?

Do you imagine the snake slid in close before closer,
　　　left conjuring rot and cracking the stillness?

Do you think for a minute I didn't think, the taste a taunt
　　　to try?

Do you recall our tongues tied thick with words
　　　as the worm from the apple surfaced?

Tell me this, before you tell me again what it is like to lie
　　　as a wolf with a lamb and not feel hunger.

The Exile

Frederic Chopin
1810 – 1849

Only shadows enter my tent
  as men pass between me and the sunset.
                            ~ Ezra Pound

1

The pride in Warsaw fails,

its absence a kind of embarrassment —
like that first lesson on your childhood piano

> when the notes ran around
> in a panic
> heavy and smudged
> the mark of a fist unpleased.

This is the story of an evening in Poland.

> Your fingers slipped
> on a fragment of time.

> A permanent dream walked
> upside down in your hands.

2

Catherine's lover,
the former King Stanislaus,
imagines crown and scepter unbesieged.

But on his throne night lies

and in the pockets of his streets
soldiers shuffle death
like a deck of marked cards.

3

What does it matter
the smoke of burning city
rising like your last audience

your cafes
conspiring in a Russian tongue

men in your beloved country
touching their women darkly?

At just the right moment
your once-denied hands
will speak to the deaf
with their own gestures.

Mazurkas will lighten your moon-starved room.

Steady as She Goes

A heart can get unsteady
waiting

for that deal with heaven
to clear

for that once-closed window
to open into revelation

for feelings
to re-jigger themselves

into a triumvirate of possibilities.

II.

Listen

Picasso once said, "To draw is to shut your eyes and sing." To write poetry, I would say, is to close your eyes and listen.

For a very long time, I knew to close my eyes but could not make the listening work. Words, even straight from the heart, went wrong, not specific enough, abstractions instead of concrete details, a holding back of what needed to be let go.

I could acknowledge that I was a writer. I made my living by my writing and my editorial skills. I relinquished the notion that I could be a poet.

Until one late November afternoon in 2007, when my brother, just two years older than I, called to tell me he had cancer and was given a timeline of weeks. I was a thousand miles away. I wanted to make matter what I wanted to say, and I wanted to hear what he had never said before.

Patrick did not die until May 5, 2009. In the interim, his cancer opened in me a need for words that could be as straight up and unadorned as his diagnosis was final, and as full an expression of love as my heart could share. After everything else had been stripped away, love was what could stand for something more.

I began to write, and what I wrote took the form of poetry, and poem after poem I shared with an online cancer support group, something I would never have done thirty years earlier. Sharing the words that illuminated my experience became the group's experience, too. The words came to be more than good enough. I learned how my voice could speak for more than me alone, and how poems could save me when, to paraphrase poet Stephen Spender, I allowed my real self to blaze through.

Cancer took the life of my brother, though not for the first time a member of my family and not for the first time someone I love.

Cancer also gave me a new voice that I'm learning to use.

Summer Headlines

In a season that gives women's names
to summer storms

Cindy Sheehan goes to court,
her crime the crossing of a line

dividing mothers from their sons.
Ten Russians, their sleepers' covers blown,

get swapped for four whose years
behind the bars wear their faces

like stripes re-lashed on prison clothes.
The French regard for scandal

brings TV to Sarkozy, who does not offer cake
where thick-tongued *bon mots* will do.

LeBron free agent takes Miami Heat
and Cleveland decries it foul.

The bulls run their mean streak through Pamplona
while oil chews its path through marsh

to shore, relentless, like the stream
of Srebrenica's green-covered coffins

borne 60,000 strong to Potocari,
Mladic the General a fugitive still.

Cloud computing's future's hazy,
Polanski's the Swiss assured. Spain beats

Netherlands in South Africa and scores
fall in Nairobi, twin blasts rocking

out in World Cup mischief. Elsewhere,
one hundred eleven naked people

wearing nothing but some sun screen
skinny dip their way into a record book

and a woman in Maine gets a class ring
back after twenty-eight years. Meanwhile,

six months since January and counting,
Haiti's homeless live and eat and sleep in streets,

like the oily pelican chicks on island rookeries,
waiting for the clean-up.

Helianthus

un tournesol: turn with
the sun and see no shadow
on a day's path traced
flowering head the whirling
worshipper of unbent light

Bearing Much Fruit

You shall know them by their fruits.
  ~ Matthew 7:16

Oranges lemons limes
grapes figs and fish

plenty of shelves stocked
for pillage before a storm

stamped in plain black
  "Inspected by _____."

What we buy we wash and rinse.
What we rinse we peel

as if removing the stain
of someone else's touch

is enough
to remove the bruises.

We stuff the fig.
We bread the fish

as if changing texture or taste
in the mouth

or leaving meat unexposed
is the better for you

and so the better for me

who pointed out with kindness
once what was could be

and always will be
before turning you free to make

your separate peace with what was
and is and might always be imperfect.

A Mother's Day
(May 10, 2009)

1

Bones-pained, she cushions herself
in a fifties-old high-backed chintz chair
rescued from some other parlor
earlier emptied of over visitations.

Before her a sleek slash of gleaming black
stainless steel, its adjustable catafalque hip-high,
enwraps in white satin the third of nine
she bore as the good wife she augured to be.

He made it to 59 (barely),
she long past that Depression generation so used
to tall-telling days when bread and stamps cost pennies
and she walked a mile, maybe two, to school.

From where she receives hands and tears
up on her seat of caned memories
— some hers, some not —
this is Mother's Day.

2

We stand and sit and re-rise, all mothers
in this tight-aired room this 90-degree day,
matriarch and daughters
still five in number, still keening

The difference calculated in a hymn of names
for a mother, a father, a son for six months,
an infant — female, delivered still —
also a husband, also, after, a significant other

And now before her riot-red eyes,
his working-man's hands tied up
in rosary beads, this son
for whom her puzzled loss cannot stand
in metered rhythms of good-bye.

3

No clock attends the hours she sits
remarking to every other guest as any woman might
how she couldn't imagine spending Mother's Day
in a Florida funeral home

A video tribute raising tunes he liked,
pictures tracing through a brain-feed
the places he'd come and left, people who'd done the same,
life's reel turned back and looping.

4

We imprint what the mind can reduce to hold:
the baby
the boy
the young adult
the middle-aged man

Married no children
friend
uncle
brother
son.

5

Her mother's heart
sadly, not without affection, recapitulates
the stories of others' stories others tell

Filling that cramped space of hush
rushed in between 4:00 and 6:00 p.m.,
picked up again after 8:00

Last chances over

All the sisters who are mothers
spelling that room.

Church

Look,
we build walls
we add pews
a bell a cross unadorned

Side by side
we collect
knit prayers on knees
raw with asking

Accept body and blood
unto our own
looking for miracles

Tell me,
if I come to the door
if the door is locked
do I wait

Look,
a door walls
pews a bell
faith changes
nothing

I can stand
out
I can stand
in

The test's the same

Upon Seeing Alice in 3D

No doubt you
have some special talent

in my dreams. Not everyone,
after all, is born

as you with such a figment
for suspended animation

so head o'er heels,
gyre and gimble in the wabe

of whiffling tulgey wood and
borogoves. But — and, mind you

there's always a but
for to reason and wrestle — I wish

you'd make your mimsy more
beware. Words lobbed

one hemisphere over another
wither sense and numbers

get turned 'round and cards
do battle white against red and

black knight banished not with love and
teapots upset and, oh dear, yes,

a rabbit dressed in morning coat
serves up no one's snicker-snack! Would

Mad Hatter had burbled on for
me as Tweedledum does Tweedledee

as he does Alice, too, and, galumphing
back behind White Queen

before the Red is dead, bow
deep and spell me, as his wont, his

eyes to spin and brain to
freeze. What more might leave you

stunned? Your drug of choice
numbs the stress and press of time

at the back of the neck like thumbs
on screws. Meanwhile, I up from hole

removed such rose-colored glasses
as Alice, herself returned quite right

in head, does her own fair bidding
best, a jib to Hatter's jig and jag of

glorious nonsense. Callooh! Callay!

Reading Goodnight Moon

is not like stopping
at McDonald's
for your favorite double-shot latte.

You don't drive through.

You take each word
in a languishing slide off the tongue,
naming what is named
that you never saw before.

Looking, finding, pointing delighted
in the room the moon the light
the red balloon that lifts

Darkness even as sleep
falls fast
and clock's hands change

What you see changing
before a child's eyes.

If you slow long enough
to take in what your child sees
with eyes that

Refuse to be moved
to a new page before
the first page is exhausted

The last page you turn
holds the dream
you thought would never last:

A snuggling close closer still
beneath moon's shadows.

To Be Re-enchanted Is Uneasy

To be re-enchanted is uneasy
with an unquiet mind
holding on to daily reminders
of what you're about to lose
you imagine you've lost already

Moment and moment and moment
clocking away unaccounted for
as you, sitting as on watch,
join sentinels all praise-worn
and too quick to gather for the left-behind
before the gone are gone

I would as soon die as miss
morning coming up, the swelling round
of cloud before lightbursts, the press
of stars to complete a night's worth of sky
for clearing dreams

To be re-enchanted is to listen
closely enough to
see near enough to
wait just long enough
for what really matters:

arriving with words let loose of rage,
gentling breaths, fingertips that know
to touch away the scrum in eyes
turned dimmer by the hour

To be re-enchanted
is to dance when no one else
can hear the music
where you are today
where I come to sing

Strong-Arming (The End of the World)

Take the day
before winter comes

to measure the distance
below heaven to earth.

Culture it in the dazzling flash
in New Mexico's desert.

Picture the forked tongue of a rattler
seeking in unforgiving ground,

tensile. Regard the stiff-eared rabbit
left red-eyed and twitching

in Alamogordo's dust. Pray what words
might be heard at the very moment

in that place on a continent far off
where the heat will be greatest.

Consider the imprecision of numbers.
Take the morning after the day of

to think through the clarity
of roughened right-angled elbows

as fingers fastened, stretched,
and gripped again. Recall the parachute

billowing. Now compute the strength
to pull up to pull back to pull off

the end of this same story
in your own hometown

after you've paced
its quiet streets at dawn.

Calculating Feelings by the Sun and the Moon

These are the facts, according to the U.S. Naval Observatory's
Astronomical Applications Department:

On June 21,
the sun rises at 5:43 a.m. EDT
and sets at 8:37 p.m. EDT.

It is the longest day of the year,
and I miss you.

Tomorrow,
the moon will rise at 5:10 a.m. EDT.

A half-hour and 3 minutes later,
the sun will take its place.

Technically, that day
will be as long as the day before

until the day after,
when, on June 23, we will
have one minute less of light.

But I will miss you all the same
and for just as long.

Exactly six months from now
time will have fallen back already.

That day will be the shortest yet.
It will be December 21.

The sun will rise at 7:23 a.m. EST
and set at 4:50 p.m. EST.

Technically,
between the Summer and Winter solstices

how I feel about you
will not be measured off

in seconds minutes or hours
not by Eastern Daylight
not by Standard intervals.

This will always be so.

Bird Lands

Sleep shakes out into *Morgenland*
   — land of morning —

stubby doves break the fast of silence
with *kwurr-kwurrs* and *woo-coos,*

sift the grass for themes to nourish
lilting songs to fill the cracks of dawn

and beat off blue-jacketed jays'
rockfest of distractions.

Magnolias blossom in *Abenland*
   — land of afternoon —

its mood rising to the velvety blue-black
of ravens' shimmery long-lined backs.

Storms are coming, the sparrows
suddenly massing, tufted heads tucked in

close to wait out the cloud-clash,
the plaint of rain on fevered blades gone brown.

Soon the all-clear, borne on a live-wire streak
of dew-nipped wings, the sharp bead of eyes

thrilling to feed in the *Land der Nacht*
   — land of night —

the hoot of echoes in a clearing
just below the upraised roof of the sky

become a decrescendo of swooping owls
taking up their night's watch

of stars splitting the dark like gone-mad cells
making work of new life.

Trial Season

Only yesterday did earth redress
its layers of browned forgotten bloom

shedding its sheath for winter with the pace
of an old man making do with a gimp left leg.

Things happen.

Spring starts up
a widespread yellow operation

braced for the challenge,
armed with emerald swords.

      Tiny eruptions
      surround themselves
      with unclaimed crowns,
      circles of fire.

It's a mystery mixing you up.

      One day the wind shakes out pollen,
      smuggled gold, gods of love;
      the next, glimmers of honey, shimmery bronzes,
      light as in the south of France.

Summer just as soon changes heart,
waves colors like the invader his banners

before committing suicide
on a city sidewalk in front of you.

Unbuttoned buds turn scarlet at the touch,
viral and infectious,
pulsing in a violet more intense than blood
in the hand squeezed with passion.

You think,
this is no big secret

     going yellow to blue to red.

You think what you like most is
the sureness of it

     how you can count on it
     coming back

     like a lover you've argued with.

8.0 at 6:48 a.m.

It registered
random images
flat dulled life-bereft

taking out
a mere few feet
above the sea

what minutes before
was waking to a day.

Tsunami
four to be exact
15-to-20-foot
ocean disturbances
smashing their ways to shore.

What do you say to the left-behind?
That God spoke there?

On American Samoa
in Pago Pago in Niua
on Tonga
as far away as Australia
half-way between
New Zealand and Hawaii

they did not have 5 minutes
from earthquake to tsunami
to get away
to run uphill
to answer fear.

The sea, you see,
is home now.

Ode to Compassion

When you are old,
re-spin me your beginnings

from their Greek and Irish
coordinates, unplot straight lines

of ancient made-up histories,
upend the stakes of claims in bindings

of your mother's mother's mother's womb
cut and spilling life into care.

When you are grey,
recall me to the look of the father

for his daughters not your sons,
your pock-mocked map we carried fixed

into our futures, cardinal points worn
dim but steadfast ever in their tending to

of place, where time's and the body's limits
join the suffering together and to death.

When you are old and grey and full
of sleep, speak to me no more of forgiveness.

On the Scene

Rubble-roughed hands reach
into what's left: the muddle of wires and masonry,
chipped, the pink paint flaking; a broken sink
a bin for books with broken spines, just so many
words caught in a dust up of bad Voodoo.

    No one would have believed
    how the ridge line would peel away,
    the lush green hills cleave, how the rains
    would come to flash-flood the ravines
    of life once got by.

From what's junk the stick at the end
of the hands catches what at first gives not,
glints, then rattles and comes clean:
the eight-year-old's jawbone, the mother's skull
stripped of flesh by dogs on the scene; hungry, too.

    No one would have believed
    how the earth would give and take,
    leaving the husband just pictures wrapped
    so carefully now in plastic, preserving in color
    what lost becomes black and white, and lies stilled.

The hands motion against the eyes
recalling the place the husband last marked
his story retold, where mangoes, bananas, and yams
ripened to sweeten a patch of land called country,
his own reduced to a tarp on a sunken football field.

No one would have believed
how ordinary death would smell,
how it would rise from collapse and float
and six months later have gone,
the shift in the air no longer
the excitement of one more body found.

The hands make a move for sleeping,
rest to be broken on a bed of scavenged wood,
listening to kompa, perhaps some Haitian hip-hop,
growing courage with a thimble of rum, setting
the dominoes right, praying fate in spray-painted graffiti
in the pause before moving on again.

Portrait by Matisse

Yours is a music
of morning sunlight:

a shaft of wheat,
also the mood of a paling moon,
the blue of the town madam on Christmas Eve.

You, poet of crayons and cutouts and glue,
dance me through October dew:

color it champagne
lighter than swallows in flight,
your thought the rest.

I slip onto your easel dressed in the scarlets
of mad words and love's open sores.

Even when you set me against a background
not exactly white, men smile at me,

The laughter in your hands contagious after all.

That Noise in the Waiting Room

More than once
it happens —

the outbreak —

a tittering "sorry"
at the particular mangling

of the name calling,
after some late arrival

rushes the front desk
half-clothed, making heads

and the registrar's brows
rise like orchestra players

paying homage
to the guest conductor

just as the papers shuffle
and time moves off

schedule and you want
so badly to think

that's just not funny.

The waiting does it
to the nerves

makes the pulse mock
the tension, the room's silence

imploding before a needle
uneasily jabbed

into tapped-on skin
finds its mark

and the hand releases
the fist and the mask

fitted not to bruise
sends oxygen on its way.

The face and the body
do it

together, involuntarily

under certain conditions,
not faked, so naturally

it's called the best
medicine no one gets

yet

making 15 muscles in the face
contract and your upper lip

to lift and you to gulp breaths
and water to pool in your ductwork

and your mouth to open and shut
like a set of teeth set loose

on Intake's counter, the security
window closed to the sight of looks

reddening, moist, the more air
fails to get in.

It's so quick
in the time you hear it

it's gone and disappeared

its punctuation effect
contagious, lighting up

the whole brain
every 210 milliseconds —

right hemisphere and left cortex,
the frontal lobe, sensory processing

in the occipital lobe, the motor
sections — and 30 times more likely

when you're not alone

and the joke's good enough
and the operation, the third already

that morning, is the success
you've sat listening for.

Pictures of Patience

1

Fingers lace
a human bandage
to hide the blues
and yellowed purples
committed to cover
biding the clock's
sweeping hands
the tapping gently
9 - 1 - 1

2

When you're hungry
listening
takes fearsome patience
a coyote's dirt-scraped crouch
the rotation of
owl-eyed gestures
the snap-to
of a rattler
seconds before striking

3

Luck's meter
the day after the day after
depending on the cards
falling just so

4

Numerals on a forearm
do not shift with time
the way memory
unhinges with a drag
in the story's telling

Almonds Are Falling

Nature has no meaning; its events are not signs.
    ~ Philosopher Susan Neiman, Evil in Modern Thought

Ready-packed the pallets rise.
Relief backs up for
another try   for another line
for another day.

Fortified biscuits   powdered
milk   rice   whole red beans
water so precious
a drop lost is like a prayer.

Dry food goes down
like dust.

Almonds are falling
in church yards

crushed
stepped over
stepped around

too many
to gather
to remember their names.

What lingers to make
new connections
floats to the sea.

They climb a hill
who can, reach
out who must.

Hope spends itself
in effort.

Effort spends itself
in promise.

Promise is a boat
going nowhere.

A basket, bottomless,
takes a miracle
to fill.

III.

Exit

Every good-bye is a provocation, an invitation to witness an ending and claim it aloud. The ending may last hours, days or weeks, months or years, before it changes back to a beginning that restarts everything with hello. Or good-bye may stretch into time that has no name.

Sometimes, how we respond to an ending is second-nature. We wake to the slant of light in our room or to the sound of the alarm. We rise and dress, pour coffee, and kiss the one we love good-bye, matter-of-course, lips out, eyes open.

We can greet the provocation with like ending. Add a hug or a handshake, and seal its meaning. Withhold it, turn sharp, and walk away, pronouncing it finished and unutterably over, never showing the stinging tears.

We can change the provocation by changing the words we use. Not just "Good-bye" or "So long" or "See you" but "I'll miss you while you're gone" and "I'll see you soon" and "I can't wait for you to come home."

Intentions marry our words to action.

Death levels every good-bye. It leaves us to wonder what was the last word heard, how was it proffered, how was it accepted, did it matter after the eyes closed and the breath soughed.

I've said a lot of good-byes, but those I've written are the ones I look to, to survive.

Senses

What is it like,
this knowing that your days are numbered
like some calendar we keep to recall where we've been
but not to forget where we are now?

If we look from your eyes,
what would we see beyond the leaf-like veins
tracing their paths to growths once cut away
like mold from cheese gone bad?

If we listen with your ears,
when would we hear the falling away of breaths
against the time you choose to speak
your final last ever words forever?

If we dare not get close enough,
how would we smell the char of lungs
burned hands brain numbed,
your flesh made Holy Ghost?

If we sit at your table,
could we taste the biting salt of loss
immeasurable as the grains of sand
washed up on the beach you love?

If we take your hands in ours,
might we somehow touch the spot where feeling
of sister for brother and mother for son
begins and ends then begins again?

Words Take On Such Color Paled

for Diane W.

Words take on such color paled
at loss pronounced.

Morning's skittering revelry
strikes dulled notes.

The evening's looks
hold webs of grief unsaid.

Spin them
thread to thread
in silence.

His hand
now falls to you
with love.

Of His Image

You,
lying too tired now to care
how time strikes in the wrong direction.

Pewter hair, strand by strand
collecting on your pillow like evidence dust,
the DNA of no crime but cells
that have abandoned you.

Morphine's drip lullingly loosens
a sequencing of dreams
stilling the jazz in your brain.

A single drug-spiked line curries no
bewilderment at the exact moment
your life slips from manageable to untenable:

It's its own instant gratification.

I see your house shuttered against the prying:

Your wife, unsheltered inside,
resolves to quit the phone.
Your dog carries the heaviness
of silence corrupted in the sway of its back.

Florida's sun sears the grass where fall
browned palm fronds curling fetal-like,
soon to be ash to mark God's sign
that once you in his image conjured

Some stripped-down version of prayer
to deliver us all from this evil.

Radio Therapy

Many people with cancer need radiation therapy . . . Sometimes,
radiation therapy is the only kind of cancer treatment people need.
  ~ National Cancer Institute

Before the radiation
can begin its slow and steady burn,

before it can stop or shrink
or cure the growth,

they have to take certain steps
to protect you.

You give yourself up
to these ministrations,

certain you have chosen
the lesser of pains you imagine.

The simulation scheduled,
you know what to expect:

face en-meshed, the mask attached
to a table to keep your head in place,

holes cut away
for eyes and nose and mouth

(Does it hurt less this way?
Provide enough air?)

Colored-ink dots on your treatment field,
a body mold to hold you perfectly still.

It's zeropoint. Reddest bursts crisply beamed,
the enemy the target of a precise machine.

Brain stuff — a little fear, you concede —
fuzzies the signals you want to give off.

But you keep coming back
five days a week for five weeks,

Then five weeks more.

You get in the correct position,
you breathe as you always do.

You eat enough calories, take care
of your skin, drink plenty of fluids,

look for new bruises lumps bumps
swelling rashes or bleeding.

After the course has run its course,
you begin to hear whispers of an old refrain:

containment has yet to prove itself
when war is called for.

You don't mention this effect.
You don't want them to think you're a loser.

You cannot feel hear see or smell radiation.
They don't always know what will work.

For the rest of your life you prepare
to come back for follow-up care.

One day they tell you the mass is gone.
One day they tell you it's everywhere.

Grounded in Fall

I missed fall
that evening

you called at 7:30
with your out-of-the-blue news.

The heat wasn't on
yet.

Your numbing words
ice-picked

the dead silence
at my end.

But for the tears collecting
like ratty edged leaves

the rut of stinging lines
streaking each cheek

I'd have screamed
for Thanksgiving's early arrival.

You so matter-of-fact
at having it all this time

no one knowing
not even guessing

when we all met up
that past last May

and took our turn
in your top-down T-bird

exclaiming the chance
to slow down before advancing

the shift in gears
smoother for once

not unlike the unrelenting pace
of cell division you'd left

to the wheel of fortune
already rigged to slow

as the circle begins
to complete itself.

Not hearing
from you

was never unusual
so much as just like you.

We got down to business
me asking, you telling

the time to be left
maybe six weeks

meaning you'd be dead
before Christmas.

How were you to know
saying it would change it

giving you one more year
before the slide

back downhill
into another fall

leaving you room
to prepare the ground

and us reason enough
not to believe

what the doctors said.

Heartfelt

Pain isn't a wound
    we can stitch
    to a close

The way we patch
    the hole a bullet makes
    or lace the skin that bones pierce.

Pain rises between
    the gaps left behind
    for the mind to wander in

And tears, when they come,
    get swapped for words we've learned
    to speak only to ourselves.

Our hearts pull
    blood in before
    pushing it out.

Measure pain slowly,
    wait for it to dull,
    offer it time and memory.

Border Crossing

Your eyes hold the memory of breath
held back at the crossing of borders:

the sucking in before the hush,
throat muscles tight and twinging

while lungs fill with the ticking fear
the guards always hear

just before you present your papers.
You soften their gaze,

hoping to hurry the line along,
mime the part of the person they want

you to be: not a woman,
not with child, not a scarf wrapping

your head filled with veiled visions
of dining on sweet plums and eggplant

just before shoes empty of souls
in the jam of market stalls

fate's likely to make the morning's news.
Yours is not the last name exclaimed;

neither is it the first that will be forgotten.
Your eyes hold the memory of breath

set free in a dream of fictions
whispered, the way truth gets stretched

across the boundaries of imagination
you'd readily give up to strangers,

the way you know you'll give up prayers
in the places where they work.

Last Words

Have you ever wondered
at the last words of a dying man?

Yours, not directed to me,
came second-hand:

Well, you got what you wanted.

Baptism secured,
the storm of out-of-control cells
done with

You dream into another place.

Merciful hospice nurses
tuck away the wrinkles

Of the sheets enrobing you
like an alabaster shroud.

At the foot of your bed
they tend a votive candle,

Its light shadowing
a picture of our father
and your wedding ring.

Grief's Lessons

for Patrick

I've learned to rock my grief
    inside, the way a doctor's fingers,

all rubber-gloved smoothness, gently massage
    the chest cavity open before reaching in to expose

the raw fist-sized metronome that keeps
    keeping our time perfectly, even after

the skin cracks and the bones, ossified,
    turn porous and hollow, more a sieve

for questions than a sarcophagus for answers
    used up in memories refusing to anchor

the past. I've learned to check for light
    in the darkness, not unlike drinking too much

cheap red wine and trying to make out the stars
    studding Orion's belt or tracing the imprint

of your head on the pillow, wondering ever after
    who got the last word, how a thousand miles away

I could be left in the stillness
    just as the call came breaking the morning's shine.

Breaking It Off:
Letter from Anne Sexton

It is not enough
I have waited, a woman
with her knees bent to the dawn?

I slept with your promises, too,
welcomed them like I did
the slit of your eye on my back.

I celebrated with an empty nightgown
in a bed too big for two,
seclusion the gift of *Lucky Strikes,*
my vodka my booze.

Like a madman aflutter I nursed
nightmares in my arms,
rocked them to sleep, baby,
picked at their meaning
till my knuckles bled.

Your name hoarse in my throat,
I swallowed whole days
woven of hunches, hard-guessed
the rumors delivered in pieces.

God, you can be so cold.

When you needed oxygen,
I buried my lips
in your good right hand,
our habit of words never easy.

You covered my eyes
with your insistent kiss
and still I could see
I was losing you.

Tonight I get to watch
the pall of roses
failing at my window.

The Message

Silence bears in and bears down,
enveloping you like waves
first sucking you under
before taking you back to shore.

Sometimes, the air just heaves with it,
filling rooms once loud with words
and laughter with a different voice
from a different place you've not grown used to.

Sometimes, it simply draws in on itself,
not persuaded by your invitation to leave, persisting
even as light through a trinity of windows
accents more than a temporary possibility.

Patient, silence waits to give up
the answer to understanding what's left
once you've been given over to
another's invisible hands.

What It's Like

for Laurie S.

The feelings of loss come
    at the sight of his old empty shoes

        mail without his name
        Christmas cards addressed only to you

The feelings of loss come
        with the sound you hesitate to erase
        from your answering machine

        the voice of the friend
        who's never heard he died

        the last words that fail to stop
        that ringing in your ears

The feelings of loss come
        because the dog gives up waiting

        seasons cycle through again
        flowers start up once more

The feelings of loss come
        because emptiness has a way
        of sticking around

You have to tend feelings—and loss—carefully

You box with shadows
You fill in space
You leave lights on

Paradise

To live where the ocean
is a step away
might be something to want
but for your sake.

In your paradise, sand collects
a grain for a grain for each passing hour
you measure in no particular rhythm.

As you lie confined, un-uttering,
un-impressed by some sign on the horizon
proclaiming your work done,

agaves slice the scented air,
their thick green blades lengthening
as your day lengthens.

No end in sight.

Do you dream, as I do, of your dying?

In your paradise, dreams
I tell you,
can lift the dark straight up

like the tropical palms
outside your window
swaying and scratching the sky.

Do you hear the song I sing?

Alligators' bark, sea cows' plaint
dolphins echoing your sixth sense
of danger waiting in your paradise:

coral snakes' glint, vultures' moody eyes
parrots' mad flutters, saw grass wheezing.

Temptation's run its course.

You're running yours.

Ode to Grief

Grief's a shiv
in the heart, held

like free verse
rocking in the mouth

as a mother her babe
rocks lullingly

forth and back
meaning to repeat

the patterned
picking up and putting down

of solid markers
drawn like the longest

lines in the palms
of the hands

twinned to
close up to open out

till life and death
fold in

along skin-cracks
in the core

once more
beginning to heal

with the air you take in

The Art of Japanese Paper Folding

I will write peace on your wings and you will fly all over the world.
~ Words written by Sadako Sasaki on 644 paper cranes she folded that
could not save her life from atom bomb disease but became a symbol for peace

At *How Hour* in Hiroshima
Sadako Sasaki was two years old.

She could not have dreamed
on August 6, 1945,
of meeting Colonel Paul Tibbets

nor ever have prepared enough
for the flash of *Little Boy's* arrival
on the *Enola Gay.*

10 feet long, 28 inches in diameter,
8,900 pounds, approximate,
this never-before-tested design —

its possibility in the conversion
of roughly 600 milligrams of mass to energy —
absolutely guaranteed to work.

> *I will write peace on your wings*
> *and you will fly all over the world.*

The National Cancer Institute estimates
that 1 of 77 men and women will be diagnosed
with leukemia during their lifetime.

Of some 43,050 new cases diagnosed,
21,840 will die.
Sadako Sasaki didn't have a lifetime.

She did get another 10 years.

Publishing its own figures on the power
of nuclear fission of uranium-235,
the United States Army guessed the following:

66,000 killed directly
69,000 injured to one degree or another
100,000, probably, dead by year's end.

In the Department of Energy's accounting
of blast, fire, and radioactive fallout —
not mentioning lingering and long-term effects —
the five-year death total might have reached
or even exceeded 200,000.

It was a complicated pattern
of destruction
of a pristine target:

Success reported
with much enthusiasm.

Twenty-five years later, Nixon presided,
and we declared a War on Cancer.

Reports are the patients are winning this one.

In the x-ray heated air, at 8:15 a.m. JST,
Sadako Sasaki didn't stand a chance
against atom bomb disease.

She lived one-and-a-half miles
from Ground Zero.

Explaining risk, the National Cancer Institute
says children who survive exposure
to very high levels of radiation
from atomic bomb explosions are much more likely
than others to get leukemia.

Running a race in 1955, sixth-grader Sadako Sasaki,
age 12, collapsed.

On February 21, she entered the hospital.

> *I will write peace on your wings*
> *and you will fly all over the world.*

In Japan, the *tsuru* is a national treasure,
a sacred symbol of honor and loyalty,
fidelity, good fortune, longevity.

Her best friend told Sadako Sasaki
the greatest wish is granted to the person
who folds one thousand cranes.

Sadako Sasaki's one wish was to get well.

So she began folding cranes —
no cuts, no glue —
each fold a step toward
longed-for recovery.

In Japanese fables, immortals ride
around on cranes.
In reality, mortals fly planes that leave behind
a shadow permanently etched
in the stone steps near a bank building.

A child's fingers, like an arthritic woman's,
can be all thumbs, refusing to obey
the mind's commands.

Sadako Sasaki's flowed with kinetic energy,
even as her blood worked the ending of her story.
So she wished instead for world peace,
safety from the effects of war.

> *I will write peace on your wings*
> *and you will fly all over the world.*

Sadako Sasaki folded 644 cranes
making the smallest number of folds possible.
She could not reach *senbazuru* on her own.

Classmates thus also folded
paper with hope, folded paper for healing,
their 356 more cranes all buried with her.

"Most cancer is not born but made," claimed
a *Washington Post* article on November 4, 2007.
"It's time to admit that our efforts have often targeted
the wrong enemies and used the wrong weapons."

In Hiroshima's National Memorial Peace Park,
in an open field created by the equivalent
of 13 kilotons to 18 kilotons of TNT
capable of taking 140,000 lives,
Sadako Sasaki stands in bronze,
her arms cradling a golden crane,
tsuru: national treasure, sacred symbol.

"This is our cry, this is our prayer, peace in the world."

I will write peace on your wings
and you will fly all over the world.

I will fold one thousand cranes
and pay watchful waiting forward.

Final Exit on a Grace Note

Let us celebrate with sweet words
the lifting of the scrim before the promised Eden

re-sound the perfectly pitched grace notes
pricking our stranded memory's retreat

into one and then another rosary
one bead to count every earlier misfire

in that thinnest of places we wanted for respite.

Let us celebrate with wine
the occasion transfigured before the flash

of the eighth day of creation
when stripped broken and hungering

we kneaded dough from yeast enough to redeem
the work of another's hands upon our own.

Out of the once lumps of clay let us carve
a single line of shimmering grace

in the crevice of belief.

Let us repeat the pattern of sonorous words
put down on vellum and fed us like formula

from a simple silver cup.

From our lips plumped red
comes the miracle:

the chattered communion of ash with dust.

IV.

Remember

Memories are like scraps of paper on which you've scrawled a couple of words you think will spark an image later or help you recall a time or a place you might otherwise have lost.

The time, once gone, you always want to recover. You fix it with its date on your calendar, the way each mile you travel on a highway gets fixed with a number staked in the ground, so that even as you move forward you know how far you've come.

The place becomes what your mind makes of it. Given enough time, it becomes, inevitably, something else. It becomes what you cannot return to, because what made it your memory no longer exists.

The image you want to deepen over time, to re-place in your mind time and again what you hold there, so that you hold it stronger still. It helps if you can look at a picture that has a before but no after.

For weeks after my brother died, every day became a date fixed on my calendar, a toll of time spent, every new hour another marker beyond the hour that a single candle at the foot of his bed burned bright until it did not.

For months I could hear his voice during his last phone call to me. A thousand miles away, and it was clear: what we both knew and would not say.

The place Patrick is now is not the place I've reached in his absence. The first year has had its anniversary, and night has opened again and again into morning. I cannot hear now more than I committed then not to lose.

What I committed not to lose was not his being but his going. That, I scrawled on scraps of paper that exist today in another form in the heart of my computer. I can see what I can call up at will, what the memory chip preserves: so many words that made images and poems that give nothing but a name to a sister's love.

Neruda's Memoirs

1

Che Ernesto Guevara carried poems and pistols.
Neruda's cantos ran with his blood
in a Bolivian jungle. They played like bullets
in the soldiers' backs.

2

Neruda said the closest thing to poetry
is a loaf of bread
or a ceramic dish
or a piece of wood lovingly carved.

So he poured his words
into the glass of another language
only some of the world speaks.

He gave light to the mines of Coquimbo.
Now they glitter like dew on a silver fish.

He left the smell of fresh ink and crisp paper
at the broker's, who traded his wife's voice
for a rainbow of lightning.

He melted the snow on broad-sided mountains
to water the dust on Santiago's tongue.

He found the blue of Chile's sky
in the bellies of volcanoes, its silence
in a guitar in Spain.

Neruda's the rush of roots
after a sudden breath

the warm tear on a face in love

the sound of adolescence missing a beat.

3

The sea could rise above him;
the wind make a sail of him.

He was too young
for the blackness of his dress,
the year climbing to its close.

But when asked,
the poet shaped in the man
remembers a ride on an empty road
and the color of rain in his childhood
and the look of a long-necked swan
that would not sing when it died
heavy in his arms one undone afternoon.

4

Meanwhile, his name;
the time and place adventure traced.

This would be Neruda:

a diary of shorelines
a journey of borrowed phrases
a work of nights, alone/together.

His heart followed a habit to a stranger's land.

In Paris people uncovered their heads
to feel the daylight of his words.

New York strung its darkness before him.
Stockholm made him an expensive diploma.

Later, medals marched across his chest
and men in high places
shook his hand like a walking stick.

5

The life of a poet is all a disguise.

In the eyes of a woman
Neruda is the ceremony of an open palm.

6

Neruda wove the gaps in his life
into tapestries he hung around the world.

In his own country they shimmer
like lies before the firing squads.

Human Scale

Thirty years
107 floors, 110 stories

defying clouds

North and South
beacons and shadows both

ordinary miracles of engineering
landfill

steel scraping
an evening's worth of stars

a favored device
to frame the Hudson

or caress a shimmer of sky.

These windows on the world

this city's emblem
that dependable backdrop

our milestone markers
once

they stood for and against.

Then it was Tuesday
and God held his breath

and our selves smalled
looked up

looking back.

We Can Remember

Wafting roasting chicory root
steam-driven café au lait
beignets by fistfuls
on a randy French corner.

Serendipity's tune
getting loose from back pockets
in a Bourbon Street dive

and Jean Lafitte look-alikes
making the rounds
as day broke day
by day.

A jumble of shrimp and crab
oysters and crawfish
curried and bisqued
for a magician's pittance
— or a dreamy pirate's scowl.

White columns stretching
to hold the shade
for southern belles' beauty
on morns too-bright
with hissing Bayou heat.

The storm coming
the water rising
the levees crumbling
the refinery leaking
the wondering squall
of need

for everything
worth having.

Watching eyes watching
for hope
getting lost in hope
never arriving

early enough
or at all.

We can remember: loss
granting no claim
on those who
could forget
would still forget
do forget

a city
a ward
a block
a house
a home

troubled by mud
mold-stormed and mucked
stuck in the caw
of some southern politician's memory.

It was a place to be
once

where po' boys
might speak
some approximation
of lazy French

and delicate young ladies
wave triangles
of fine lace hankies
to their suitors' sway

where a river channeled
gained its own control
over man's made things

and not even bleach
could recover
what water rinsed
what water washed
what water wasted in.

Enough

Where do we take cover
once the dying's done?

To name the pain
is not enough
to push what's deeper forward.

We have to learn again
to bare our hearts
to bear our grief

To make refuge within ourselves
respite from the catechism
practiced daily, bedside.

Feelings, not being felt
the way we finger rosary beads,
don't fall into line so neatly.

Words can't mimic nor hands mime
what we look for in the red swirl
yet to stain our thirsting lips.

Nothing Is Ever the Same

Not the *brrringing* of the telephone
when you record the message

Not the favorite restaurant
where every table is fixed with two chairs

Not the bed,
one side, not his: hers

Nothing is ever the same

Not the coffee, not the tea
grounds staled, leaves foretold

Not the car
keys dangling
hooked fast like a mouse in owl eyes

Not the vase of iris
its water run low again

Blue-purple tongues taking bows
in a finger's drift of pollen

Nothing is ever the same
or could be the same

After you left

After you left
dust on your collections
hats, books, scraps
of half-thought dreams unbound —

Piled on

As time piled on
to keep me busy unforgetting

The nothing that is never the same
when your name no longer gets called

Sore Chasing Dreams

Sore with chasing
dreams, I scatter

fresh-bought seed
in un-neat rows.

Ravens, wheeling
through cotton-balled clouds,

show me the meaning
of passion

at ground level.

A Feeling Grew Into a Hope

A feeling grew
into a hope.

It started out
a worry whorled

the way a conch
flips and turns

until out
goes inside

and deep
hard-shelled

feeling becomes invisible.

Out of warm waters
ocean's pink-lipped horn

trumpeted the sound
of tears evaporating

in motions chiming
to the heart's recovery.

Garden

Trees are Earth's endless effort to speak to the listening heaven.
  ~ Rabindranath Tagore

Too soon summer strikes itself at end.
The gathering collects.

The full of fear
hesitate at the garden's gates,
not prepared to recall
the language of oaks and elms,
maples and sycamores,
walnuts and tupelos,
sweetgum and willow.

The seekers — of what
they cannot define —
scatter seed the ground welcomes,
intent to find their way.

A few step well beyond
the paths to claim,
etching their mile markers
with the names we keep before us.

Not to forget
we do not forget.

Simply to say:
They were here. They are with us. They hear.

We all shelter in hope against loss.
Fall, nearer now, will have its way.

Color drawn first to brilliance
itself will fail, falling out of range
of keenest eyes
and moon whose thickness
once was guide enough
will stretch the merest strip of shine.

Hardwoods shorn of green
will stand a reminder
of what we only sometimes
reach with words.

Grant Me the Wish

Grant me the wish to walk your road
    smooth again

        to clip the path free of such moments
            as only the young have

        to believe without question
            no life is fixed in a certain direction.

Grant me the wish to hear in your words
    not who I am not yet

        but who I might be in such moments
            as only the young have

        to forget the obstacles to yes
            because the heart beats right.

Grant me the wish to need you
    no more nor less

        to claim in such moments
            as only the young have

        to offer the lot of themselves
            even if just fragments exist.

Grant me the wish to draw for you
    one perfect circle close

        around us in such moments
            as only the young have

        to uncontain the infinity that hides
            in all the space between.

No Easy Solace

No easy solace
comes

by treasure
both moth and rust consume.

The heart contused,
it gives no solace

to memory once blacked
and blued.

Love
its light from star or moon

crocheted
as from a spider's womb.

What Is Enough

Blessed are they who are thankful,
for they show us what is enough.

Legs twig-thinned, toes splayed,
you balance crumbed morsel
nit-picked ground to beak

and wait on
no more

blessing with skittered trillings
the handout
of a hand out.

You watch
for the anticipation,
the nodding pause

of giving
being its own best thanks.

See me. *See* me. See *me.*

It is enough
to be in this world
to be of it

to render unto Caesar
what things are God's alone

to give

to stand
the cobbled stone of earth

tender cracks
filling up
filling in filling out

the questions caught in eyes

making peace
with enough.

In Will's Real Place

As memory chinks fall away
and the mouth holding

its now full-hushed voice
agitates to give them life —

remember the way, once, hurled
from the end of an acid-etched tongue,

words burned through skin and bone,
cleaving protective muscle —

as all you can hear, besides
the cut-off and clicking on again

of well-calibrated but unseen gauges
steadying temperature for others' convenience

and the constant thrum
of overhead tubes of too-white light

breaking time with the soft-padded grip
of nurses' shoes moving room to room

to take the evening's counts.
Who is more than a thought makes you

company, salves your palsied hand
with lavender-enriched potions

to draw from you the yesterday
lost to cells' destruction?

In this place a bracelet round the wrist
holds some key to your identity

better than your mind
the reassurance we're still here.

Your chart accepts the numbers
tallied methodically with every slip of response

failing the newest most aggressive
treatments. Still, we check what we can

leave behind in so unfamiliar a territory,
which whispers in your good right ear

fix you with character enough to rally
chapter and verse against a thinning stream

of spittle, let you run your course here
where a decision made months and years ago,

signed and dated and stamped,
settles how it would end as your end came near.

Worn Shirt

I never told you how I saved
the shirt our father wore
the afternoon he died.

Stuffed in a brown paper bag
some nurse handed me as I wound
through and out Emergency,
leaving him behind.

The whiteness of that shirt:
it wasn't new, it wasn't old,
it was his. I put it to my nose

guessing at the number of hours
it had touched his back,
wondering at stitching still in place,
considering the beating his heart took.

Late that July evening I folded his shirt
as though it were my husband's own
and put it on my closet shelf.

Almost 20 years it lay unclean,
secreted in a pitch of dark,
as our father is,
as you soon will be.

Twenty-Two

for ddb

Twenty-two's no famous route number,
no too-broad sticky-surfaced strip of tar

tamed with double solid lines down the middle.
Your road, though not unshouldered, takes you

another year to reach and I want to ask
how does it wind uphill all the way

away from me. On a single-digit day
this day one August past, who else but I

decried more loudly your coming of age
decreed with inks and etching pen?

The threshold of your arrival not to be
put off, you hopped your long board

on some corner in the Village where I, in rain,
watched your muscled, thinned-down frame

— shirtless, so the wind couldn't hold you back —
get lost among wheeling orange cabs and hawkers

of ripped-off *Chanel* bags, and took in a single look
back in the always-turned-on, never-sleeping city

framing fascination in your eyes. Tomorrow
I'll stand holding open the door to the street,

keeping an eye out, and like an old love come back
to haunt you, feel my heart growing and growing still.

Lately I Am Missing You

My hand's a list of lines I work to follow
beginning to end. The result's always the same.

Like trying to print with marks etched in a copper plate
too many times inked and pressed or cut too deep,

my mind refuses, is yet to yield to one more effort to trace
and imprint my image of you as our father's favorite son.

My sense of you grown cold and too soon strange, what I have
left is tears I count, just so many beads in grief's necklace

I finger in remembrance, stuttering your name the way I did not
as I called to God to answer the day

your chart would yield no clue. Absence all and everywhere
at once wants for definition.

Pulling Thread

To mend
is to pull
thread tight

Just right

Long stitches
short
short stitches
long

A pattern made
enough is
enough
to hold me
close
enough

Stranger in Town

Ft. Myers
Sanibel-Captiva

More than a thousand miles away
it is high noon.

The sun, an orange fist in a still life,
goes public.

Clouds sticky as new wet plaster
accept the glare here.

Bodies heat up fast as irons,
pull shifts on sand like men on maneuvers.

Straight as matchsticks,
palms let the wind do their talking.

They sway seductive
as belly dancers, slithery-trunked, easy.

I tell you
innocence is not what it was.

I tell you
the moon sheds lovers now and again.

The Gulf, warm as water in the womb,
rocks me, but not clumsy, not any old way.

After so much disorder, it sends me ashore
better than an old bottle with a forgotten message.

In this place are no motels
pressing you to sleep

no trinket shops
pitching for a sell.

The land leaves you alone here.
Men and other women leave you alone.

A thousand miles away,
I would tear down a star to give you

Send you a scarlet leaf,
some thing that counts the days till Christmas.

But summer's got its hold on.

Today I understand
what it means to come back.

Spring Thaw

Heads up:

tiny shoots

break earth's shell

spring up

from winter's

bed of dreams

showing us

how to make

a comeback

every time

Acknowledgments

I dedicate this collection to my brother Patrick William Doallas (March 25, 1950 – May 5, 2009). Because of him, I started writing poetry again.

I could not have continued writing during my brother's experience of cancer were it not for my friends at Our Cancer, a number of whom have not lived to celebrate with me what this collection means to all of us. To you, therefore, I return the gift of "I see you" and pay my gratitude forward to: Laurie S., Laurie H., Al, Stan, Ned, Joyce H., Dianne, Kim, Betty, Sasha, Michael, Kathie S., Mully, Sue C., Ron, Fay, and the Big Guy responsible for the place we never wanted to visit and still can't leave, Leroy Sievers.

Special thanks go to my friend Randall David Tipton, whose paintings show me how the sureness of His hand in another's can pull color from the blackest black and leave us laughing in a riot of red or enthralled in a mood of blue.

When I began blogging in late September 2009, I never imagined I'd end up becoming part of a group of online writers and poets who hold Twitter poetry jams and tie countless knots that hold tight the threads of connection I maintain all over the United States, Canada, and now Europe and beyond. Always generous with their comments about my poems and other writings, the following deserve a calling out, too: L.L. and Marcus whose support and belief in me made this book possible, Glynn, nAncY, Diane W., Louise, Joyceann, Jenne', Christine, Sunrise Sister, Lucy, Roberta, Jan R., Kathy a.k.a. "katdish", Eric, Brad, Laura B., Bridget, Brad, Sam, Sarah E., Kathleen O., Jay, Cass, Anne, Ann, Leslie, Melissa, Deborah, Billy C., and Kelly. Any omissions are not intentional and if you think you belong in this company of encouragers, you do.

Never last on any list of mine is my husband Jim. To him, I offer my deep appreciation and love for giving me both the space and time to write and think and write some more, without once having to worry about earning my keep.

Also from T. S. Poetry Press

Barbies at Communion: and Other Poems, by Marcus Goodyear

Marcus Goodyear's poems are portable, easily carried in the mind, tightly compressed and deceptively simple, like a capacious tent folded into a package you can tuck in your backpack.

— John Wilson, Editor, *Books & Culture*

From Barbies to tea bags and credit cards, from broken pipes to communion wafers and mowing dead grass, Marcus Goodyear moves us through our world. His juxtapositions of the conventionally sacred and profane reveal to us the falsness of our conventions. Where the vision is large, all is sacred.

— John Leax, author *Tabloid News*

God in the Yard: Spiritual Practice for the Rest of Us, by L.L. Barkat

Mix Richard Foster and Annie Dillard in a blender, and you'll pour out *God in the Yard...*

— Ginger Kolbaba, editor Christianity Today's *Kyria*

L.L. Barkat's wise words move us more deeply into matters of consequence.

— David Naugle, author *Reordered Love, Reordered Lives: Learning the Deep Meaning of Happiness*

Available in e-book and print editions

www.ingramcontent.com/pod-product-compliance
Lightning Source LLC
Chambersburg PA
CBHW030006110426
42736CB00040BA/519